# THE AMERICA
# AT SALCOMBE A ___ ___ ___ ___
# DURING WORLD WAR TWO

## Revised edition

Copyright ©
ORCHARD PUBLICATIONS 2005

Originally compiled by Muriel and David Murch and Len Fairweather in 1984 and
published by Arthur Clamp

ORCHARD PUBLICATIONS
2  Orchard Close, Chudleigh, Devon TQ13 0LR
Telephone: (01626) 852714

ISBN  1 898964 66 1

*Printed by*
Hedgerow Print, Crediton, Devon EX17 1ES

# Contents

# ACKNOWLEDGMENTS

The bulk of the photographs used in this book came from the wartime collection of the late Lieutenant Commander Francis Murch, Royal Naval Volunteer Reserve and we are greatly indebted to his two sons Francis Murch and Arthur H. Murch for making them available to us.

W. Dotson of Rochester, U.S.A., kindly brought his wartime photograph album for us to copy. Martin W. Vincentsen, another wartime 'visitor' to Salcombe, also gave permission to reproduce his collection of photographs and documents. Dr. Ralph C. Green, M.D., of Chicago, allowed reproduction of the damaged Landing Ship Tank photograph. Other photographs were loaned by Mr. and Mrs. Hirschberg, Robert Chapman and Arthur Clamp and given to us by Mrs. Wilson and Mrs. Lethbridge. We are also grateful for the assistance of the Imperial War Museum for their help and use of their photographs; to the Chief of Information, Department of the U.S. Army, Washington D.C.; to Norman Glason for his excellent map, and Mr. and Mrs. J. J. Petit for the use of their wedding photograph. Copyright of the B.B.C. Hulton Picture Library photograph is acknowledged: threshing machine, page 35.

Muriel and David Murch and Len Fairweather.

For this revised edition Orchard Publications also acknowledge Robin Rose-Price and Jean Parnell for the use of photographs previously reproduced in *The Land we left behind* and *400 years in Torcross - a Pictorial History*.

Above: Commander William H. Henszey U.S.N.R. Commanding Officer U.S.N.A.A.B., Salcombe.

Left: Lieutenant (later Lieutenant Comander) Francis Murch, R.N.V.R. Resident Naval Officer, Salcombe. Awarded American Legion of Merit, 7th September, 1945.

4

# INTRODUCTION

The inhabitants of the South Hams little realised how the arrival of Winston Churchill in Quebec on 13 August 1943 for conferences with Mackenzie King, the Canadian Prime Minister, and President Roosevelt would affect their lives. The 'Quadrant' conference between the three men and their staffs, held a week later ended with a decision to prepare for a 'second front' against Germany in France which would be codenamed 'Overlord'. The first front being Operation Husky - the invasion of Sicily by British and American forces in July, 1943, followed by the invasion of Italy a few weeks later. At that meeting final plans for the provision of shore facilities, which would be necessary to train personnel, maintain and repair landing vessels, supply and store all war materials needed for a successful landing on the French coast, were discussed and agreed. In September, 1943, a United States Naval Construction Battalion (Seabee's) moved into Salcombe to establish an Amphibious Base. The following month the Americans moved into Dartmouth and set up the Amphibious Forces Training Centre No. XI.

At Dartmouth the build up of United States personnel reached a total of 3,684 officers and men, about 2,000 of whom were accommodated in the Royal Naval College, 880 in huts, and an unfortunate 462 in tents, all in the college grounds. Local houses were requisitioned for the remaining 434. The Royal Naval jetties and workshops provided most of the harbour facilities.

The arrival of 137 officers and 1,793 men at Salcombe had a greater impact on the inhabitants than twice the number did at Dartmouth. The Americans were to outnumber the depleted wartime population of Salcombe. They took over the Salcombe Hotel and about sixty other properties. On the hill above the town Quonset huts (oversized Nissen huts) were erected. St. Elmo Hotel became a hospital; the lower part of Cliff House was used as a galley and mess hall, whilst the upper rooms were used for instructional and recreational purposes. Opposite the Victoria Inn, derelict cottages were bulldozed down, to make a slipway and loading ramp. On Millbay a concrete slipway was built, complete with launching trolley and winches capable of hauling the larger Landing Craft Tanks out of the water for repair and maintenance. The local roads and lanes became congested with vehicles bringing in supplies and materials.

On 16th November, 1943, notices were posted in Slapton, Strete, Blackawton, East Allington, Sherford, Stokenham and Torcross, informing the inhabitants that the area had been requisitioned by the Admiralty. Everyone had to be out by 20th December. Although it was not stated at the time, the area was similar to parts of the French coast where the invasion of Europe would be spearheaded. In this area lived nearly 3,000 people including many farmers with their farm animals. The main problems for each family were: Where could they obtain sufficient boxes and packing cases, which would be necessary to shift all the household and personal items? What could be done with the carefully hoarded stocks of rationed winter fuel and where could they go? Farmers had the additional problems of finding new grazing land outside the area or selling their animals for slaughter, plus moving machinery and crops stored in barns and ricks and those still in the ground. The civilian organisations, both national and local, got down to the task of helping and advising. Assistance in evacuation was given by personnel from the Royal Navy and the American Army and Navy.

Just before Christmas 1943 it was announced that General Dwight Eisenhower had been appointed Supreme Commander of the Allied Expeditionary Force preparing for the invasion of France. A few days later it was further announced General Montgomery would be his ground force commander.

From the middle of March until after D.Day all non-military traffic was stopped between southern England and the rest of the United Kingdom. The roads were congested because troops and their equipment were moving to assembly points close to their embarkation ports. From April civilians were prohibited from visiting any part of the coast between Norfolk and Cornwall. The prohibition of photography was rigidly enforced.

While the naval vessels were serviced for the last time, the Royal Air Force and United States Air Force were keeping up their harassment of the enemy. From Dunkeswell in east Devon, 110 Squadron specially equipped anti-submarine Liberator aircraft were patrolling the channel.

During the last days of May, 1944, the rumble of tanks and military vehicles, interspersed by the clumping of army boots, was heard throughout the day and night as the Allied forces moved to board the invasion craft. By 1st June all vessels were fully loaded and awaited orders to sail. Poor weather prevented sailing on the planned date, but on the evening of 4th June, 1944, the vessels sailed out of Salcombe Harbour to join others for the attack on occupied Europe which commenced in the early hours of the 6th June.

Whilst all hell was let loose on the other side of the channel, the South Hams was strangely empty and quiet. A small number of Americans of the advance Port Party remained with their gear. Their task was to clear and then operate the port of Cherbourg once it was liberated. The Germans stubbornly held on thus forcing the Allies to continue to use the prefabricated Mulberry harbour and to re-open the Salcombe repair depot, which continued to function until the end of the war in Europe.

The task of clearing the Slapton training area of explosives took a long time. Unfortunately a lot of unnecessary vandalism was perpetrated by people living outside the area before the original inhabitants were permitted to return. Some, having found new homes, never did return.

# SALCOMBE

On 29th September, 1943, No. 8. Egremont Terrace, Devon Road, was the first house to be requisitioned and occupied by United States Naval personnel. On the same day parts of Cliff House gardens were taken over. Cliff House assembly room was used as a mess hall and other rooms were taken for educational and recreational purposes. During the next month many more properties were occupied. For a full list of premises requisitioned see page 48.

On the hill above the town Quonset huts (oversized Nissen huts) were assembled on undeveloped land adjoining Kingsale Road, St. Dunstans Road and Camperdown Road and in the adjacent Salcombe Rugby Field.

The Salcombe Hotel became the headquarters for the United States Navy Advanced Amphibious Base. The Seabees constructed huts in the hotel grounds.

LEAVING FOR FRANCE

ADVANCE PORT PARTY

↑ ME IN MiddlE

JACK - M - RAUB - DIRENZO - GUINN - GREEN - MIKE

The Advance Port Party of U.S.N. Seabees made their way down Salcombe Hotel steps to be ferried out to their invasion craft. They were due to land and operate a French port. The war moved too quickly and the port was by-passed. The main party sat on their sea bags, played baseball and waited.

Following the invasion damaged craft limped back to Salcombe for repair and subsequent further service. The main task was LST repairs. A floating dock was moored off Ditch End and craft were winched up onto the Mill Bay slipway.

Some two weeks before D.Day Audrey Steward married Petty Officer Pharmacist Mate J. J. Petit. Audrey was the first local girl to marry an American serviceman stationed at Salcombe. Standing by the bride is Lieutenant Commander F. Murch, R.N.V.R., resident Naval Officer. With the groom is his commanding officer, Commander W. H. Henszey, U.S.N.R.

U.S. President Franklin D. Roosevelt died in April, 1945, and a memorial service was held in Salcombe Parish Church. Before the impressive service a U.S.N. trumpeter sounded 'Church Call' outside the west door of the church.

Captain R. Hunt and Captain McManus with the Salcombe Base
Commander, W. H. Henszey, met at the Salcombe Hotel to discuss the
preparations for D.Day.

V.E. Day, 8th May, 1945, in Fore Street, Salcombe, with flags flying from nearly every window.

A non-denominational thanksgiving service took place in Cliff House grounds on Sunday, l3th May, 1945, to celebrate the cessation of hostilities in Europe.

Civilian and military dignitaries stood in front of the war memorial for the 'Victory in Europe' parade. From left to right:-Chairman of the Salcombe Urban District Council, A. Boon; a Lieut. R.N.V.R. Lieut. Comm. F. Murch, R.N. V. R. Comm. W. H. Henszey, U.S.N.R.; Lieut. Col. P. Cottle, Home Guard; Ft. Lieut. Phillips R.A.F.; Sect. Officer McLean W.A.A.F. and an A.R.P. ofiicer.

Opposite. On l lth May, 1945, before the U.S. Navy left Salcombe, there was a farewell gathering in Courtenay Park. It was stated by the Base Commander that much had been underdone, much overdone, but they (the Americans) had done what they came for. There would be much to talk about and remember.

He conveyed their deepest gratitude to all and in particular to the R.N.O. whose often repeated, "We're one Navy," was under-scored by his efforts and co-operation.

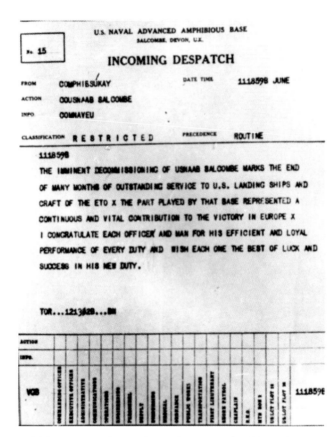

On 11th May, 1945, a congratulatory despatch was received by U.S.N.A.A.B. Salcombe from Commander of Amphibious Forces U.K.

The unveiling of 'Normandy Way' plaque at Salcombe on 4th June, 1955. Those present were Rear Admiral Charles H. Lyman, U.S. Naval Attache, London; Rear Admiral H. J. B. Grylls R.N.; Lt. Com. F. Murch, R. N. V. R., H. F. A. Wallace, Chairman Salcombe Urban District Council and E. Distin Vice-Chairman of the council.

# SLAPTON

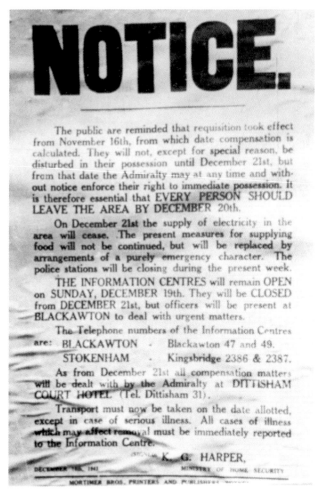

# NOTICE.

The public are reminded that requisition took effect from November 16th, from which date compensation is calculated. They will not, except for special reason, be disturbed in their possession until December 21st, but from that date the Admiralty may at any time and without notice enforce their right to immediate possession. It is therefore essential that EVERY PERSON SHOULD LEAVE THE AREA BY DECEMBER 20th.

On December 21st the supply of electricity in the area will cease. The present measures for supplying food will not be continued, but will be replaced by arrangements of a purely emergency character. The police stations will be closing during the present week.

THE INFORMATION CENTRES will remain OPEN on SUNDAY, DECEMBER 19th. They will be CLOSED from DECEMBER 21st, but officers will be present at BLACKAWTON to deal with urgent matters.

The Telephone numbers of the Information Centres are: BLACKAWTON - Blackawton 47 and 49.
STOKENHAM - Kingsbridge 2386 & 2387.

As from December 21st all compensation matters will be dealt with by the Admiralty at DITTISHAM COURT HOTEL (Tel. Dittisham 31).

Transport must now be taken on the date allotted, except in case of serious illness. All cases of illness which may affect removal must be immediately reported to the Information Centre.

K. G. HARPER,

DECEMBER 1941. MINISTRY OF HOME SECURITY

MORTIMER BROS. PRINTERS AND PUBLISHERS

On 4th November, 1943, Sir John Daw, Chairman of Devon County Council, was informed by telephone that the Slapton area was to be evacuated completely by 20th December. The area was to be requisitioned under the Defence Regulations and Compensations Act of 1939.

Sir Hugh Elles, Regional Commissioner responsible for the movement of large numbers of civilians in the South West, arranged two meetings at Exeter on 8th November. He met local councils and voluntary bodies to inform them of the plans and the problems involved. Then he told the local clergy that the evacuation of six parishes, some 3,000 people and an area of 30,000 acres had to begin at once. The area would be needed for at least six months.

# IMPORTANT MEETINGS

The area described below is to be REQUISITIONED urgently for military purposes, and must be cleared of its inhabitants by DECEMBER 20th, 1943.

Arrangements have been made to help the people in their moves, to settle them elsewhere, and to advise and assist them in the many problems with which they will be faced. To explain these arrangements

# PUBLIC MEETINGS

## will be held as follows :

### FRIDAY Nov. 12th

11 a.m.
**EAST ALLINGTON CHURCH**

2-30 p.m.
**STOKENHAM CHURCH**

### Earl Fortescue, M.C., The Lord Lieutenant
in the Chair.

### SATURDAY Nov. 13th

11 a.m.
**BLACKAWTON CHURCH**

2-30 p.m.
**SLAPTON VILLAGE HALL**

### Sir John Daw, J.P., Chairman Devon County Council
in the Chair.

These general meetings will be immediately followed by special meetings to discuss the problems of farmers, who are requested to remain behind for them.

IT IS VITALLY IMPORTANT to every householder that he should arrange to attend whichever of these meetings is nearest to his home, and where necessary employers of labour are requested to give their work-people time off for this purpose.

# THE AREA AFFECTED

ALL LAND AND BUILDINGS lying within the line from the sea at the east end of Blackpool Bay in Stoke Fleming parish to Bowden ; thence northward along the road to the Sportsman's Arms ; thence west along the Dittisham-Halwell road to the cross-roads ¼-mile east of Halwell village ; from this cross-road along the Kingsbridge road to the Woodleigh-Buckland cross-roads ; thence along the road Buckland, Frogmore, Beeson and Beesands to the sea, but excluding the villages of Frogmore, Beeson and Beesands. The roads forming the boundary are outside the area.

The parishes involved are the whole, or almost the whole, of Blackawton, East Allington, Sherford, Slapton and Strete, most of Stokenham, and parts of Stoke Fleming, Buckland-tout-Saints and Halwell.

MORTIMER BROS. PRINTERS AND PUBLISHERS, TOTNES.

He attended all the public meetings held to explain the situation to the shocked villagers and the need for U.S. troops to practice assault landings. After four years of war that they would be contributing towards the success of the Second Front when it was launched, was their only consolation. In January Sir Hugh Elles praised the villagers for the way they had coped with their lot and the efforts of the helpers concerned with the task of evacuation.

On l6th August, 1943, the first landing exercise took place on Slapton Beach when the Royal Navy put ashore American soldiers of Company 'M' and the Headquarters Company of the 175 Infantry Division. The soldiers established a beach head and landed vehicles. Wire matting was laid on the beach to prevent the wheels of the jeeps sinking into the shingle. This exercise was a very peaceful affair as no live ammunition was used and, thanks to the Royal Navy, the Americans got ashore without getting their feet wet.

The troops marched past the ruin of the Royal Sands Hotel. It had been badly damaged as the result of a black and white dog named Pincher running into the minefield laid at the beginning of the war when invasion by the Germans was a possibility. The hotel became a complete ruin during subsequent American exercises.

On 5th November, 1943, before the local residents were informed of the evacuation another landing was carried out on Slapton Beach.

Some of the 'invaders' did a little scouting and found the Queens Arms. The landlady, Mrs Lavers, dispensed hospitality to the locals and American G.I.s.

Clarence Mitchelmore, George Steer and Bill Blank discuss the problems of the evacuation with the Slapton policeman Constable Betts and two American G.I.s.

Constable Betts, a local girl and three American soldiers in Slapton village.

Mrs. Mitchelmore and her son Dennis pack their belongings. The major problems for the housewives were where to go, where to get containers to pack all the household goods and what to do with carefully horded stocks of winter fuel and food.

For the younger generation like Milwyn Mitchelmore and his cousin Basil there was the distraction of watching an American soldier stoking a field kitchen.

The three boys cannot believe their luck. Because of food rationing sweets were a real treat.

The farmers had to decide what to do with their cattle and sheep and the crops that were still in the ground or in clamps. Some managed to double up with farmers outside the area, others had to sell their animals at specially arranged markets. Everything had to go including the steam traction engine and thresher, essential equipment for a farmer at that time.

Hay-ricks were protected with thatch, in the hope that they would survive until the farmers were able to return to their farms. Root crops had to be dug up and many other tasks were carried out.

Bunks were brought to several houses which accommodated American soldiers who were on perimeter patrol to prevent unauthorised entry into the battle training area.

Soldiers helped to carry carvings and treasures from the churches. They filled sandbags which were piled up to protect church furnishings which could not be moved such as fonts, pulpits, doors and windows. At each church the following notice was displayed:

> *To our Allies of the U.S.A. This church has stood here for several hundred years. Around it has grown a community, which has lived in these houses and tilled these fields ever since there was a church. This church, this churchyard in which their loved ones lie at rest, these homes, these fields are as dear to those who have left them as are the homes and graves and fields which you, our Allies, have left behind you. They hope to return one day, as you hope to return to yours, to find them waiting to welcome them home. They entrust them to your care meanwhile and pray that God's blessing may rest upon us all.*
> *Signed*
> *Charles, Bishop of Exeter*

The W.V.S. did stirling service providing meals for all. Many voluntary bodies were involved with helping the villagers. The Civil Defence, British Red Cross and the Home Guard to name but a few. Many Ministry Departments were involved also. Naval photographers and surveyors recorded and valued property. Sailors helped with evacuation and also helped the W.V.S.

Machine guns were set up to be ready for subsequent landing exercises.

The precise area evacuated as detailed on the first notice shown on page 28 reads: - ALL LAND AND BUILDINGS lying within the line from the sea at the east end of Blackpool Bay in Stoke Fleming parish to Bowden; thence northward along the road to the Sportsman's Arms; thence west along the Dittisham-Halwell road to the cross-roads ¼ mile east of Halwell village; from this cross-road along the Kingsbridge road to the Woodleigh-Buckland cross-road; thence along the road Buckland, Frogmore, Chillington, Beeson and Beesands to the sea but excluding the villages of Frogmore, Beeson and Beesands. The roads forming the boundary are outside the area.

Following D.Day the first of the villagers to return to their homes took up residence on 15th September, 1944.

# SLAPTON EXERCISES

In the Slapton Battle Training Area many exercises were carried out before D.Day. The first amphibious exercise being Exercise Duck, 31st December, 1943, to 2nd January, 1944. There was bombardment of the beaches by four British Hunt Class destroyers under the command of Captain V. E. Korns, R. N., and landings were made by many troops of Force 'LT' who were to be the initial assault force on Utah Beach.

**Exercise Fox:** 10th to 12th March. Bombardment by two cruisers and eight destroyers.

**Exercise Muskrat:** 24th to 27th March. Bombardment by two cruisers and U.S.S. Bayfield (Rear Admiral Moon).

**Exercise Beaver:** 29th to 31st March. Bombardment by two cruisers and four destroyers.

**Exercise Trousers:** 11th to 13th April. Details not known.

**Exercise Tiger:** 26th to 29th April. Bombardment by two cruisers and seven destroyers.

**Exercise Fabius:** 3rd to 6th May. Bombardment by U.S.S. Augusta, H.M.S. Glasgow and nine U.S. destroyers.

Some of the exercises were witnessed by high ranking officers including General Eisenhower and General Montgomery and V.I.P.s including Winston Churchill.

Once the beach had been secured by the infantry, more equipment was brought in.

As the practice battle continues the LSTs land the heavier equipment

Blackpool Sands was a landing stage for fuel supplies as the exercises continued.

The engineers also needed to refine their skills so a pontoon bridge was built across Slapton Ley.

## Exercise Tiger, April 26-29th 1944.

Landing ships and landing craft left Plymouth, Dartmouth and Brixham loaded with men, vehicles and ammunition intent on landing on Slapton beach as a full rehearsal for Operation Overlord which was to follow a few weeks later.

Everything went pretty much according to plan with the first wave landing safely and moving inland and setting up a command post. However, the second wave of attacking forces which left Plymouth twenty hours later were attacked by a flotilla of nine German E-boats, carrying torpedoes and cannon. The E-boats, based in Cherbourg, left their harbour under cover of darkness on a speculative patrol of the English Channel around the Isle of Wight and Lyme Bay. A few hours later they happened upon the allied patrol. Despite being picked up on radar by the destroyer HMS Onslow, on patrol off Portland Bill, the E-boats launched a devastating attack.

At 2.00am Landing Ship Tank 507 was hit by a torpedo and burst into flame. Minutes later LST 531 was torpedoed and exploded. LST 289 witnessed the devastation and although taking evasive action had its stern blown away by another torpedo hit. Despite having lost its rudder LST 289 managed to limp back into Dartmouth. Because of a typographical error causing confusion over the radio frequency, warnings from HMS Onslow did not reach the LSTs in time for them to summon help.

The official United States toll of dead soldiers and sailors was 749 although other sources of information and research have stated the number was in excess of 1,000.

Despite this attack by the German E-boats, Exercise Tiger continued with all the undamaged LSTs completing the planned assault and landings on Slapton beach, many officers being completely unaware of what had happened a few hours earlier. As news of the disaster emerged a security restriction was imposed for fear of damage to morale with D.Day being so close. Servicemen were threatened with court-martial if they talked about it and many were transferred to other units away from Devon. Despite rumours few locals got to hear of what had occured. One story which is still talked today is of mass graves being dug inland from Slapton. However, other publications; make reference to bodies being taken from Weymouth in Dorset to cemeteries up country. Certainly many of the wounded were taken to hospitals in and around Weymouth and Sherbourne.

Major General Raymond O. Barton, Commanding General, Infantry Division, issued instructions during Exercise Tiger, when vessels of Rear Admiral D. Moon, U.S.N. Force 'U' from Plymouth, Salcombe, Dartmouth and Tor Bay, and troops of the 7 Corps, 4 Infantry Division and 1st. Engineer Special Brigade were involved. The troops and equipment embarked in the same ships, and for the most part, in the same ports as they would for the actual D.Day landings. The invasion fleet was protected by an outer patrol of two destroyers, three Motor Torpedo Boats and two Motor Gun Boats. Following the bombardment by two cruisers and seven destroyers, landings were made during the morning of 27th April and unloading continued all day.

The full scale of Exercise Tiger can be appreciated from the number of vessels within Start Bay, standing off Slapton Sands. Landings took place all along the beach with Torcross being protected by barbed wire in front of the village.

The follow-up convoy of eight Landing Ship Tanks due on the morning of 28th April were intercepted by nine German E. Boats. L.S.T. 507 was struck by a torpedo and caught fire. The survivors abandoned ship. A few minutes later L.S.T. 531 was hit by two torpedoes, rolled over and sank. L.S.T. 289 opened fire on the E. Boats which retaliated with a torpedo hit. Twelve men were killed but the landing craft managed to make Dartmouth harbour.

The enemy action caused consternation amongst the Allied leaders with D.Day only six weeks away. However it was decided to go ahead with the final exercise code named Fabius.

Landing Ship Tank 289 arrives back in Dartmouth showing clearly the extensive damage caused by the E-boat's torpedo.

| Taken on. | Premises: | **Particulars of U.S. Naval Accommodation, Salcombe .** |

**Particulars of U.S. Naval Accommodation, Salcombe .**

| Taken on. | Premises: |
|---|---|
| 29.9.43. | No. 8 Egremont Terrace. and Lower lawns, Clifl House. |
| 1.10.43. | The Glen, Sandhills Road, 10 rooms. |
| 14.10.43. | Jarvis Quay, Island Street and Foreshore, Shadycombe Creek, with area of waste land and access road.; Nos. 1-2-3 and 6 Mannings Boathouse. |
| 22.10.43. | Sandhills, Sandhills Road, 3000 sq. ft.; Site 8000 ft. situated at junction Camperdown and Loring Road for Hut Camp 2. ; Nos. 4 and 5 Mannings Boathouse; Council Housing Site, 1800 sq. yds, for Hut Camp 1; Lower Tennis Courts, Onslow Road, for Laundry; Portion of Cliff House and front garden; Scoble Bungalow, 4 rooms. |
| 23.10.43. | Salcombe Rugby Ground with Club premises for Hut Camp 1. |
| 1.11.43. | Fort Charles Garage; St. Elmo Hotel, 40 bedrooms; The Haven, East Portlemouth; The Little House, Portlemouth; Ferry Hill, Portlemouth; Millbay House, Garden room; Portion of Millbay foreshore; Sunnyridge, East Portlemouth; 43 acre south of Camperdown Road for Hut Camp 2; ½ car park and 1 lockup at Central Garage; Central Garage Annexe Service Station; Unity Hall, Union Street; Thornings Garage and forecourt with 2 petrol pumps and 3 oil cabinets (excluding portions requisitioned by W.D.); Dornom's Quay; Kings Arms' coal store; The Welcome Club, Island Street. |
| 2.11.43. | Second part of Cliff House; Great Gate Hotel, 17 rooms. |
| 6.11.43. | First floor flat, Cliff House. |
| 7.11.43. | Tideway, Folly Lane. |
| 11.11.43. | Garage adjoining Kings Arms' coal store; Easternmost Garage, Kings Arms' car park and western half of car park. |
| 12.11.43. | Powderham Villa, Devon Road, 9 rooms; Cotliss, Devon Road, 9 rooms. |
| 15.11.43 | Top floor, Marine Hotel and S.E. lounge lower ground floor, 17 bedrooms. |
| 23.11.43. | Castle Point, 3500 sq. ft.; Glenthorne, Devon Road, 12 rooms; Somerset Villa, Devon Road, 8 rooms; The Moorings, Devon Road, 8 rooms; The Hollies, Devon Road, 11 rooms; Oaklands, Devon Road, 9 rooms; Edinburgh House, Devon Road, 9 rooms. |
| 26.11.43. | The Institute, Devon Road, 9 rooms; Salvage Depot Kings Arms' car park; First floor store rear of Kings Arms. |
| 30.11.43. | Marine Hotel, 1435 sq. ft.; White Strand Quay and demolition of public lavatories; Area of land approx ¾ acre of arable and 1¼ acres of pasture, O. S. 209 Devon Sheet 136.13. cemetery site; Salcombe Hotel, 70 rooms, garage and car park over basement annexe. |
| 25.12.43. | Two Hoots car park, Nos. 3 and 4 lockup garages with portion of car park with open-fronted shed thereon. |
| 30.12.43. | Area of pasture being Pt. O.S. No. 21 1 Devon Sheet 136.15, ammo site; Stonehanger Garage, 1350 sq. ft. |
| 7.1.44. | ¾ acre rough grazing bounded on the South by Kingsale Road and on the West by St. Dunstans Road together with 3 enclosures of pasture having frontage of approx. 280 ft. to Kingsale Road for Hut Camp 2. |
| 18.1.44. | Site for U.S. signal mast at Scoble Point. |
| 20.1.44. | Hannaford's loft. |
| 21.1.44. | Remainder of Central Garage and Store at Custom House Quay. |
| 22.1.44. | No. 10 Mannings Boathouse. |
| 1.3.44. | Western National Bus Depot; Cooks Store, 76 Fore Street; J. C. Dornom Bros., 72 Fore Street, for U.S.N. Post OfFice, 3 rooms. |
| 8.4.44. | No. 1 Cliftonville, Devon Road, 9 rooms; No. 5 Courtenay Terrace, Devon Road, 9 rooms. |
| 1.5.44. | Yard surrounding Hannaford's loft. |
| 18.5.44. | No. 9 Mannings Boat Store. |

All properties were derequisitioned during July and August, 1945.